THE POLITICAL HORROR
BOOK

THE
POLITICAL BEATS WITHIN THE STATES

Don't let them continue to be our nightmare

CALEB MAINA IDI

THE POLITICAL BEASTS WITHIN THE STATES

Don't let them continue to be our nightmare

TABLE OF CONTENTS

Chapter 1

Introduction:

Political beasts within the states refer to individuals who possess a deep understanding of the political landscape and use their knowledge to influence political decisions. These individuals are often well-versed in political theory and have a keen sense of strategy and tactics that they use to advance their political goals. In this article, we will explore the definition of political beasts within the states, their historical background, and their significance in contemporary politics.

Definition of Political Beasts within the States:

Political beasts within the states are individuals who possess a deep understanding of the political landscape and use their knowledge to advance their political agenda. They are often skilled in the art of political strategy and tactics and use these skills to influence political decisions. Political beasts can be found in all levels of government, from local city councils to national governments.

Political beasts are not necessarily tied to a particular political ideology or party. They may be conservatives, liberals, socialists, or any other political persuasion. What distinguishes political beasts is their ability to navigate the political landscape and achieve their objectives, regardless of the political environment.

Historical Background and Significance:

Political beasts have been a fixture in politics since ancient times. The Greek philosopher Aristotle wrote extensively about politics and the importance of understanding the political landscape. Machiavelli, in his famous work The Prince, also emphasized the importance of political strategy and tactics.

In modern times, political beasts have become even more important. As the political landscape has become increasingly complex, it has become more difficult for politicians to achieve their objectives without the help of skilled political strategists. Political beasts are often employed by political parties, interest groups, and other organizations to help them achieve their goals.

The significance of political beasts in contemporary politics cannot be overstated. They play a critical role in shaping political outcomes and influencing policy decisions. Without political beasts, it would be much more difficult for politicians and interest groups to achieve their objectives.

Political beasts within the states are individuals who possess a deep understanding of the political landscape and use their knowledge to advance their political goals. They are skilled in the art of political strategy and tactics and play a critical role in shaping political outcomes. The historical background of political beasts dates back to ancient times, and their significance in contemporary politics cannot be overstated. Understanding the role of political beasts is essential for anyone interested in politics or public policy.

Chapter 2

The Nature of Political Beasts:

Political beasts are individuals who are driven by a desire for power and influence within the realm of politics. They may seek elected office or work behind the scenes to exert their influence. These individuals are often highly motivated, competitive, and willing to use any means necessary to achieve their goals. The nature of political beasts is shaped by a complex array of factors, including personal ambition, ideology, cultural context, and historical precedent.

What Defines Political Beasts?

At their core, political beasts are defined by their unrelenting pursuit of power and their willingness to engage in ruthless tactics to achieve their goals. They are often highly skilled at networking, manipulating, and persuading others to support their objectives. Their ultimate aim is to gain control over the levers of power within a political system, whether that be through elected office, appointment to key positions, or behind-the-scenes influence.

Characteristics of Political Beasts:

Political beasts share a number of key characteristics that distinguish them from other individuals in the political arena. These include:

Ambition: Political beasts are driven by a deep-seated desire for power and influence.

Strategic Thinking: Political beasts are highly skilled at strategic thinking, and are able to anticipate the likely consequences of their actions.

Charisma: Political beasts are often charismatic individuals who are able to inspire others to support their goals.

Ruthlessness: Political beasts are willing to use any means necessary to achieve their objectives, including manipulation, deceit, and intimidation.

Resilience: Political beasts are able to bounce back from setbacks and setbacks, and are able to adapt their strategies to changing circumstances.

Opportunism: Political beasts are skilled at identifying opportunities for advancement and exploiting them to their advantage.

Types of Political Beasts:

There are several different types of political beasts, each with their own unique characteristics and motivations. These include:

The Ideologue: The ideologue is driven by a deep commitment to a particular ideology or set of beliefs, and seeks to advance these beliefs through political means.

The Pragmatist: The pragmatist is more concerned with achieving practical outcomes than with adhering to any particular ideology. They are highly skilled at compromise and coalition-building, and are able to work across party lines to achieve their objectives.

The Opportunist: The opportunist is motivated primarily by personal gain, and is willing to switch sides or change their positions on key issues if it serves their interests.

The Machiavellian: The Machiavellian is highly skilled at manipulating others to achieve their goals. They are willing to use deception, intimidation, and other underhanded tactics to get what they want.

The Populist: The populist is a charismatic leader who seeks to mobilize popular support for their agenda. They often present themselves as outsiders who are fighting against the established political elites.

In conclusion, the nature of political beasts is complex and multifaceted. They are defined by their unrelenting pursuit of power and their willingness to engage in ruthless tactics to achieve their objectives. Political beasts share a number of key characteristics, including ambition, strategic thinking, charisma, ruthlessness, resilience, and opportunism. There are several different types of political beasts, each with their own unique characteristics and motivations. Understanding the nature of political beasts is essential for anyone seeking to navigate the complex world of politics.

Chapter 3

Political Beasts in US

Political beasts have been a prominent feature of US politics since the nation's founding. These individuals are characterized by their intense ambition, fierce determination, and willingness to do whatever it takes to succeed in the political arena. While some may view them as necessary for progress and success, others see them as ruthless and destructive to democracy.

A Brief History of Political Beasts in the US:

One of the earliest examples of a political beast in the US was Alexander Hamilton, who was one of the country's founding fathers. Hamilton was fiercely ambitious and wanted to establish a strong central government that would be able to address the country's economic problems. He was involved in numerous political conflicts during his lifetime and was eventually killed in a duel with political rival Aaron Burr.

In the early 20th century, another political beast emerged in the form of Franklin D. Roosevelt. FDR was a master politician who was able to use his charisma and political skills to push through major reforms, including the New Deal. His presidency spanned four terms, making him the longest-serving president in US history.

In the 1960s, Lyndon B. Johnson also exhibited political beast-like qualities. He was a master of political maneuvering and was able to push through major civil rights legislation, including the Civil Rights Act of 1964 and the Voting Rights Act of 1965.

The Role of Political Beasts in US Politics Today:

Today, political beasts continue to play a prominent role in US politics. These individuals are often highly skilled at fundraising, networking, and building coalitions. They are often willing to take risks and make controversial decisions in order to achieve their political goals. However, they can also be highly divisive and polarizing, and may be seen as contributing to the growing political polarization in the country.

Examples of Political Beasts in US Politics:

One of the most prominent political beasts in recent US history is Donald Trump. Trump was able to capture the Republican nomination and win the presidency in 2016 through a combination of charisma, media savvy, and willingness to break with traditional political norms. He was a highly divisive figure during his presidency, and his legacy continues to shape US politics today.

Another example of a political beast is Alexandria Ocasio-Cortez, who was elected to Congress in 2018. AOC, as she is often called, has become a vocal and influential figure on the left, advocating for progressive policies such as the Green New Deal and Medicare for All. She has also shown a willingness to take on the Democratic establishment and push for more radical change within the party.

In conclusion, political beasts have been a fixture of US politics since the nation's founding. While they can be highly effective at achieving their political goals, they can also be highly divisive and polarizing. As US politics becomes increasingly polarized, the role of political beasts in shaping the political landscape is likely to continue to be significant.

Chapter 4

Political Beasts and Governance

Political beasts, also known as political power brokers or kingmakers, refer to influential individuals or groups within the political sphere who wield significant power and influence over government policies, decision-making, and leadership. The impact of political beasts on governance can be both positive and negative, depending on their intentions, values, and methods.

One way in which political beasts influence governance is through their ability to control the selection and appointment of political leaders, including presidents, prime ministers, and other high-ranking officials. By leveraging their financial resources, networks, and support base, they can endorse or campaign for candidates who align with their interests, and ensure that those who are elected or appointed owe them a debt of gratitude. This can result in the appointment of capable and experienced leaders who are capable of advancing the national interest, or it can lead to the elevation of inexperienced or corrupt leaders who prioritize their own interests over those of the public.

Another way in which political beasts influence governance is through their ability to shape public opinion and discourse through their control over the media, social networks, and public relations. By framing issues in a particular way, disseminating selective information, and mobilizing public opinion, they can sway policy decisions in their favor, or block the implementation of policies that they oppose. This can result in the adoption of policies that benefit the majority of the population, or it can lead to the adoption of policies that favor a small, elite group of individuals or corporations.

The positive impact of political beasts on governance is often seen in their ability to mobilize resources, networks, and support for development projects, social welfare programs, and poverty reduction initiatives. By leveraging their political power and influence, they can attract investment, promote entrepreneurship, and create job opportunities, which can help to alleviate poverty, reduce inequality, and improve the standard of living for the population. They can also use their influence to advocate for the protection of human rights, civil liberties, and democratic principles, which can help to promote the rule of law and good governance.

However, the negative impact of political beasts on governance is often seen in their ability to perpetuate corruption, nepotism, and cronyism, which can undermine the integrity of government institutions, erode public trust, and weaken democratic processes. They can also promote policies that benefit their own interests at the expense of the public interest, such as monopolistic practices, tax evasion, and environmental degradation, which can result in economic inequality, social unrest, and environmental degradation.

Strategies for managing political beasts include promoting transparency and accountability in government institutions, strengthening the rule of law and the independence of the judiciary, promoting a free and independent media, and strengthening civil society organizations. By ensuring that political decisions are based on the public interest, rather than the interests of a small elite group, and by promoting the participation of diverse stakeholders in policy-making processes, governments can help to mitigate the negative impact of political beasts on governance. Additionally, promoting ethical leadership, promoting anti-corruption efforts, and enforcing campaign finance regulations can also help to reduce the influence of political beasts on governance.

In conclusion, political beasts can have a significant impact on governance, both positive and negative. While they can promote development, social welfare, and human rights, they can also perpetuate corruption, nepotism, and cronyism. Strategies for managing political beasts include promoting transparency and accountability in government institutions, strengthening the rule of law and the independence of the judiciary, promoting a free and independent media, and strengthening civil society organizations. By doing so, governments can help to ensure that political decisions are made in the public interest, and that the negative impact of political beasts on governance is mitigated.

Chapter 5

The Impact of Political Beasts on Elections

Political beasts, or individuals who use manipulative tactics and aggressive strategies to advance their political goals, have a significant impact on elections. These individuals often have deep pockets, strong networks, and powerful allies, which allow them to exert significant influence on the outcome of elections.

One of the primary ways in which political beasts impact elections is by leveraging their resources to run high-profile campaigns that saturate the media and public discourse. They may use negative advertising, smear campaigns, and other tactics to discredit their opponents and sway public opinion in their favor.

Additionally, political beasts may also use their resources to mobilize voters, either through targeted advertising or by funding get-out-the-vote efforts. They may also use their influence to intimidate or coerce voters, which can suppress voter turnout and skew the election in their favor.

Overall, the impact of political beasts on elections is significant, and their tactics can have long-lasting effects on the political landscape. As such, it is essential for voters and other stakeholders to remain vigilant and informed about the role of political beasts in elections.

The Role of Political Beasts in Elections

Political beasts play a crucial role in elections, as they often have the resources and influence needed to shape the outcome of the race. These individuals may use a variety of tactics to advance their goals, including negative advertising, smear campaigns, and voter suppression.

Additionally, political beasts may also use their resources to mobilize voters and build strong coalitions that support their campaigns. They may use targeted advertising, social media campaigns, and other strategies to reach potential supporters and encourage them to vote.

Furthermore, political beasts may also play a key role in shaping public opinion about key issues and candidates. They may use their influence to sway media coverage, push certain narratives, and frame the conversation around key topics.

Overall, the role of political beasts in elections is complex and multifaceted. While they can play a positive role in mobilizing voters and advancing important issues, they can also use their influence to manipulate the outcome of the race and undermine the democratic process.

Political beasts can have a significant impact on the outcome of elections, as they often have the resources and influence needed to shape public opinion and mobilize voters. Their tactics can range from negative advertising and smear campaigns to voter suppression and intimidation.

One of the primary ways in which political beasts impact election outcomes is by shaping public opinion about key issues and candidates. They may use their influence to push certain narratives, frame the conversation around key topics, and sway media coverage in their favor.

Additionally, political beasts may also use their resources to mobilize voters and build strong coalitions that support their campaigns. They may use targeted advertising, social media campaigns, and other strategies to reach potential supporters and encourage them to vote.

Furthermore, political beasts may also use their influence to suppress voter turnout or intimidate voters, which can skew the election in their favor. They may use a variety of tactics to discourage voters from participating in the democratic process, including spreading misinformation, conducting smear campaigns, and engaging in other forms of voter suppression.

Overall, the impact of political beasts on election outcomes is significant, and their tactics can have long-lasting effects on the political landscape. As such, it is essential for voters and other stakeholders to remain vigilant and informed about the role of political beasts in elections.

Strategies for Countering Political Beasts in Elections

Countering the influence of political beasts in elections can be a challenging task, but there are several strategies that voters and other stakeholders can use to level the playing field. Some of these strategies include:

Educating voters: One of the most effective ways to counter the influence of political beasts is by educating voters about their tactics and encouraging them to critically evaluate the messages and claims put forth by candidates. This can be done through public awareness campaigns, community events, and online resources that provide voters with accurate and unbiased information about the candidates and the issues.

Holding candidates accountable: Voters can hold candidates accountable by demanding that they stick to the issues and refrain from engaging in negative campaigning or smear tactics. This can be done through public forums, debates, and other events where candidates are forced to address issues and answer tough questions from constituents.

Supporting independent media: Political beasts often use their influence to shape media coverage in their favor, but independent media outlets can help to counteract this by providing unbiased reporting and analysis of the issues and candidates. By supporting independent media outlets, voters can ensure that they have access to accurate and unbiased information about the election.

Encouraging voter turnout: One of the most effective ways to counter the influence of political beasts is by encouraging voter turnout. When more people participate in the democratic process, it becomes harder for political beasts to sway the election in their favor. This can be done through voter registration drives, get-out-the-vote efforts, and other initiatives that encourage people to exercise their right to vote.

: **Political** beasts often use their resources to gain an unfair advantage in elections, but campaign finance reform can help to level the playing field. By supporting measures that limit the influence of money in politics and increase transparency around campaign finance, voters can help to reduce the impact of political beasts on elections.

In conclusion, countering the influence of political beasts in elections requires a multi-faceted approach that involves educating voters, holding candidates accountable, supporting independent media, encouraging voter turnout, and supporting campaign finance reform. By taking these steps, voters and other stakeholders can help to ensure that elections are fair, transparent, and reflective of the will of the people.

Chapter 6

The relationship between media and politics

The relationship between media and politics has always been a complex one. In a democratic society, media serves as a watchdog to ensure that politicians remain accountable to the people. At the same time, media has the power to shape public opinion and influence political behavior. The role of media in shaping political beasts cannot be underestimated. In this article, we will examine the relationship between media and political beasts, the impact of media on their behavior, and the responsibility of media in preventing them.

Political beasts are individuals who use their power and influence to advance their own interests at the expense of others. They are driven by their desire for power and control, and they will do whatever it takes to achieve their goals. Media plays a significant role in shaping political beasts by providing them with a platform to communicate their ideas and ideologies to the public. The media can either amplify or diminish the voices of political beasts, depending on their coverage and presentation.

The relationship between media and political beasts is complex. On the one hand, political beasts need the media to promote their agenda and gain public support. On the other hand, media needs political beasts to create sensational stories that capture the public's attention. This symbiotic relationship can create a dangerous dynamic, where political beasts use the media to spread their message and gain power, while the media uses political beasts to generate clicks and ratings.

The impact of media on political beast behavior is significant. Media coverage can either encourage or discourage political beasts from engaging in certain behaviors. For example, if the media gives extensive coverage to politicians who use fear-mongering and hate speech to gain support, other politicians may be more likely to adopt these tactics. On the other hand, if the media highlights politicians who prioritize civility and respect in their communication, other politicians may be more inclined to follow suit.

Media has a responsibility to prevent the rise of political beasts. This responsibility is rooted in the media's role as a watchdog and an advocate for democracy. The media must hold politicians accountable for their actions and expose any wrongdoing or corruption. Furthermore, the media must provide balanced coverage that gives equal weight to different perspectives and opinions. This is particularly important in a world where social media algorithms and echo chambers can create an environment where political beasts thrive.

In conclusion, the role of media in shaping political beasts is significant. The relationship between media and political beasts is complex, and the impact of media on political behavior is significant. However, media has a responsibility to prevent the rise of political beasts by holding politicians accountable, providing balanced coverage, and promoting democracy. Ultimately, the media can be a powerful tool in preventing the rise of political beasts and ensuring that our democracy remains strong and vibrant.

Chapter 7

Money plays a crucial role in the world of politics, where wealthy individuals and organizations have a significant impact on political behavior and influence. Political beasts, which refer to powerful individuals who exert influence over the political system, are often motivated by their financial interests. In this article, we will discuss the impact of money on political beasts, the role of wealth in their behavior, and strategies for limiting their influence.

The Impact of Money on Political Beasts:

Money has a profound impact on political beasts, influencing their decisions and behavior. Wealthy individuals and corporations often use their financial power to sway politicians to their favor.

They can offer campaign contributions, donations to political parties, or fund independent expenditure groups to promote their agenda.

Political beasts also use their wealth to influence public opinion. They can fund media outlets, think tanks, and advocacy groups to create a narrative that supports their interests. They can also use their wealth to sponsor research or commission polls to shape public opinion in their favor.

The Role of Money in Political Beasts' Behavior:

Money is a significant driver of political beasts' behavior. It can motivate them to support policies or politicians that benefit their financial interests. Political beasts may also use their wealth to gain access to politicians or other decision-makers, which can help them further their agenda.

Wealth can also enable political beasts to gain a competitive advantage in the political arena. They can use their financial resources to run expensive campaigns, air television ads, or sponsor events that help them connect with voters.

The Impact of Wealth on Political Beasts' Influence:

Wealth can have a significant impact on political beasts' influence. Money can buy access to politicians and decision-makers, which can help political beasts push their agenda. It can also fund campaigns or independent expenditure groups to influence the outcome of elections.

Wealth can also enable political beasts to shape public opinion. They can fund media outlets, think tanks, or advocacy groups to create a narrative that supports their interests. They can also use their wealth to sponsor research or commission polls to shape public opinion in their favor.

Strategies for Limiting the Influence of Money on Political Beasts:

There are several strategies for limiting the influence of money on political beasts. One approach is to implement campaign finance reform, which can help reduce the influence of wealthy donors on political campaigns. Campaign finance reform can include limiting the amount of money individuals or corporations can donate to political campaigns, limiting the amount of money independent expenditure groups can spend, or providing public financing for political campaigns.

Another approach is to increase transparency in political spending. This can include requiring political organizations to disclose their donors or creating a publicly accessible database of political spending.

A third approach is to limit the role of money in the political process. This can include implementing public financing for political campaigns or creating a system of small donor contributions to fund political campaigns.

In conclusion, money plays a significant role in the world of politics, where wealthy individuals and organizations exert influence over political behavior and decisions. Political beasts are often motivated by their financial interests, and their behavior and influence are shaped by their wealth. Strategies such as campaign finance reform, increased transparency, and limiting the role of money in the political process can help reduce the influence of money on political beasts and promote a more equitable and democratic political system.

Chapter 8

Special Interests in Politics.

Special interests refer to groups or individuals who have a particular stake in a particular policy or decision-making process. These groups may include corporations, trade unions, non-governmental organizations, religious groups, and others. In politics, special interests have become a crucial part of the system, as they have the power to influence political beasts, i.e., politicians, to act in their favor. This influence can take various forms, including campaign contributions, lobbying efforts, and media campaigns, among others.

The Influence of Special Interests on Political Beasts:

Special interests have a significant influence on political beasts in various ways. One of the most common ways is through campaign contributions. Special interests often contribute large sums of money to political campaigns, which can give them significant leverage over the candidates. In return, politicians may be more inclined to support policies that favor their donors, even if those policies are not in the best interest of their constituents.

Special interests can also influence political beasts through lobbying efforts. Lobbyists work on behalf of special interest groups to persuade politicians to support their agendas. They may use various tactics, including providing information, making arguments, and offering incentives, to convince politicians to take specific actions.

Another way special interests can influence political beasts is through media campaigns. Special interests may use their resources to create and disseminate messages that support their preferred policies or candidates. These messages can be targeted to specific audiences, such as voters in key districts, to help sway public opinion in their favor.

Special interests play a significant role in shaping political beasts' behavior. The desire to win elections and maintain political power often leads politicians to prioritize the interests of their donors over the needs of their constituents. This can result in policies that favor special interests at the expense of the general public.

Special interests can also shape political beasts' behavior by providing them with valuable resources, such as information, expertise, and connections. This can give politicians an advantage in the policymaking process and help them make decisions that align with the interests of their donors.

Furthermore, special interests can shape political beasts' behavior by leveraging the power of the media. By creating and disseminating messages that support their agendas, special interests can influence public opinion and pressure politicians to take specific actions.

The impact of special interests on political beasts' influence can be significant. When politicians prioritize the interests of their donors over the needs of their constituents, the democratic process can be undermined. This can lead to policies that benefit only a select few, rather than the broader public.

Furthermore, the influence of special interests can weaken public trust in government institutions. When the public perceives that politicians are acting in the interests of their donors rather than the people they represent, it can erode confidence in the democratic process.

Reducing the influence of special interests on political beasts is a complex challenge, but several strategies could help address the problem. One approach is to increase transparency in the policymaking process. This could involve requiring politicians to disclose their campaign contributions and limiting the amount of money that special interests can contribute to political campaigns. Increased transparency could help to reduce the influence of money in politics and increase public trust in the political process.

Another strategy is to limit the role of lobbyists in the policymaking process. This could involve imposing stricter regulations on lobbying activities, such as requiring lobbyists to register and disclose their activities. Limiting the role of lobbyists could help to reduce the influence of special interests on politicians and ensure that the policymaking process is more transparent and accountable.

Finally, increasing public awareness of the influence of special interests on politics could also help to reduce their impact. Educating the public about the role of special interests in politics and the potential negative consequences of their influence could encourage voters to demand more accountability and transparency from their elected officials. This could include supporting candidates who prioritize the needs of their constituents over the interests of special interests.

Overall, reducing the influence of special interests on political beasts is a complex challenge that requires a multifaceted approach. Increasing transparency, limiting the role of lobbyists, and increasing public awareness are just a few strategies that could help to address the problem. By taking action to reduce the influence of special interests on politics, we can help to ensure that the democratic process remains accountable to the needs and desires of the people it is meant to serve.

Chapter 9

Impact of political parties on political beasts

Political parties play a vital role in shaping the behavior of politicians, who are often referred to as political beasts. A political beast can be described as a politician who is ambitious, ruthless, and willing to do whatever it takes to gain power or maintain their position of authority. The impact of political parties on political beasts can be both positive and negative, and it is important for political parties to manage these individuals effectively to ensure that their behavior does not become detrimental to the party's goals.

One of the primary ways in which political parties impact the behavior of political beasts is through the party platform. The party platform outlines the party's goals, values, and policy positions, and it provides a framework for the behavior of party members. Political beasts who are committed to the party's platform will be more likely to act in accordance with the party's goals and values. Conversely, political beasts who are only interested in gaining power for themselves may be more likely to stray from the party's platform and pursue their own interests.

Political parties also have a significant impact on the behavior of political beasts through the process of candidate selection. Political parties often have a vetting process that is designed to identify candidates who are most likely to be successful in winning elections and advancing the party's goals. Political beasts who are able to navigate this process successfully will be more likely to be selected as candidates, and they will be more likely to behave in ways that are consistent with the party's goals and values.

However, political parties also have the potential to exacerbate the negative behavior of political beasts. For example, political parties may reward individuals who engage in ruthless behavior or who are willing to use unethical tactics to achieve their goals. This can create a culture in which political beasts are encouraged to behave in ways that are harmful to the party's reputation and long-term goals.

To manage political beasts effectively within political parties, there are several strategies that can be employed. One of the most important strategies is to establish a clear and consistent set of values and standards for party members to follow. This can include ethical guidelines for behavior, as well as a clear set of policies and goals for the party to pursue.

Another important strategy is to create a culture of accountability within the party. This can involve establishing systems for monitoring and evaluating the behavior of party members, as well as instituting consequences for individuals who engage in behavior that is inconsistent with the party's values and goals.

Finally, it is important for political parties to cultivate leadership that is committed to managing political beasts effectively. This can involve identifying individuals who are able to balance the need for ambition and ruthlessness with a commitment to the party's values and goals. Effective leadership can help to set the tone for the party as a whole and ensure that political beasts are managed in a way that is beneficial to the party's long-term success.

In conclusion, political parties have a significant impact on the behavior of political beasts, who are often the most ambitious and ruthless members of a party. While political beasts can be an asset to a party in terms of their ability to win elections and advance the party's goals, they can also be a liability if their behavior becomes detrimental to the party's reputation and long-term success. To manage political beasts effectively, political parties must establish clear values and standards, create a culture of accountability, and cultivate leadership that is committed to managing these individuals effectively.

Chapter 10

Impact of ideology on political beasts

Ideology plays a significant role in shaping the behavior and influence of political beasts, who are individuals or groups that are deeply committed to advancing their political agenda and gaining power within a particular political system. Political beasts may be driven by a variety of motivations, including ideology, personal ambition, or a desire for power and control. However, it is the ideological dimension that is perhaps the most important factor in understanding the behavior and influence of political beasts.

The impact of ideology on political beasts is multifaceted. On the one hand, ideology can provide a clear sense of purpose and direction for political beasts, giving them a set of beliefs and values that guide their actions and decision-making. Ideology can also create a strong sense of group identity and solidarity among political beasts, binding them together in a common cause and reinforcing their commitment to their political goals. This can make political beasts more effective in achieving their objectives, as they are able to work together more cohesively and with greater focus and determination.

On the other hand, ideology can also be a source of rigidity and inflexibility for political beasts, making it difficult for them to adapt to changing circumstances or to compromise with those who hold different views. This can lead to political gridlock or even conflict, as political beasts become entrenched in their positions and are unwilling to give ground to their opponents.

The role of ideology in shaping political beasts' behavior is particularly evident in the way that they engage with the political system. Political beasts who are aligned with a particular ideology may be more likely to seek to reshape the political system in line with their beliefs and values, using a variety of tactics to gain power and influence. This might include forming alliances with like-minded groups or individuals, using media and propaganda to sway public opinion, or engaging in direct action such as protests or acts of civil disobedience.

The impact of ideology on political beasts' influence is also significant. Political beasts who are aligned with a particular ideology may have a disproportionate influence on the political process, particularly if their views are widely shared among the electorate. They may be able to shape public opinion, influence policy decisions, or even hold positions of power within the government itself.

However, the impact of ideology on political beasts' influence can also be limited by factors such as institutional barriers, opposition from other political beasts, or changes in the political climate.

In some cases, political beasts may even become marginalized or lose influence altogether if their views fall out of favor with the public or with key decision-makers.

Strategies for managing political beasts within different ideologies can vary depending on the specific circumstances and context. However, there are some general principles that can be applied across different ideological contexts.

One key strategy is to engage with political beasts in a constructive and respectful manner, even if their views may be fundamentally opposed to one's own. This can involve seeking to understand their perspective, finding common ground where possible, and working towards compromise and collaboration in areas of shared interest.

Another strategy is to build coalitions and alliances with other groups and individuals who share similar goals or values, in order to increase one's own influence and counterbalance the influence of political beasts who may be working against one's interests.

Finally, it can be helpful to work towards creating a more inclusive and diverse political system, one that is less susceptible to domination by a small group of political beasts. This might involve promoting greater participation by underrepresented groups, strengthening democratic institutions and processes, and promoting a culture of tolerance and respect for diverse viewpoints and perspectives.

In conclusion, the impact of ideology on political beasts is complex and multifaceted, shaping their behavior, influence, and strategies for managing them. While ideology can be a powerful motivator for political beasts, it can also create obstacles to compromise and cooperation, and may even contribute to political conflict and gridlock. Effective strategies for managing

Chapter 11

The Impact of Culture on Political Beasts:

Culture plays a significant role in shaping the behavior of political beasts. Political beasts are individuals who exhibit a high level of political skill and power. They use their political skills to influence others and achieve their goals. The way political beasts operate varies depending on the culture they are in. Some cultures may reward or promote political beasts, while others may discourage or penalize such behavior.

The Role of Culture in Shaping Political Beasts' Behavior:

Culture shapes the behavior of political beasts by establishing norms, values, and beliefs about what is acceptable behavior in politics. In some cultures, political beasts are admired and respected for their skills, while in others, they may be viewed with suspicion or even disdain. For example, in some cultures, nepotism and cronyism are acceptable forms of political behavior, while in others, they are considered corrupt.

The Impact of Culture on Political Beasts' Influence:

Culture also has an impact on the level of influence that political beasts can wield. In some cultures, political beasts may be able to use their skills to gain a great deal of power and influence, while in others, their influence may be limited. This can be due to cultural norms that discourage aggressive or confrontational behavior, or a culture that values consensus-building and collaboration over individual achievement.

Managing political beasts within different cultures requires an understanding of the cultural context in which they operate. Strategies that work in one culture may not be effective in another. For example, in a culture that values hierarchy and deference to authority, it may be necessary to establish clear rules and procedures for decision-making to prevent political beasts from dominating the process. In a culture that values individual achievement and competition, it may be necessary to establish incentives and rewards for collaboration and teamwork to prevent political beasts from undermining the group's efforts.

In conclusion, culture has a significant impact on political beasts' behavior, influence, and management. It is essential to understand the cultural context in which political beasts operate to develop effective strategies for managing them. By taking into account cultural norms, values, and beliefs, we can create a more effective and sustainable approach to managing political beasts within different cultures.

Chapter 12

The Impact of Ethics on Political Beasts

Ethics play a crucial role in shaping the behavior and actions of political beasts. Political beasts are individuals who are highly ambitious, competitive, and relentless in their pursuit of power and influence. They are often willing to do whatever it takes to achieve their goals, including engaging in unethical or immoral behavior. However, the impact of ethics on political beasts cannot be overstated.

The Role of Ethics in Shaping Political Beasts' Behavior

Ethics provide a set of moral principles and values that guide individuals in their decision-making and behavior. In the political arena, ethics can help to shape the behavior of political beasts by setting a standard for acceptable conduct. Political beasts who are committed to ethical principles are less likely to engage in corrupt practices, abuse of power, and other unethical behaviors that can harm society.

Ethics also play a role in shaping the reputation of political beasts. Political beasts who are known for their ethical conduct are more likely to gain the trust and support of the public. Conversely, political beasts who engage in unethical Impactbehavior are more likely to be viewed with suspicion and mistrust.

The of Ethics on Political Beasts' Influence

The influence of political beasts can be both positive and negative. When political beasts are committed to ethical principles, their influence can be used to advance the common good. However, when political beasts engage in unethical behavior, their influence can be used to harm society and advance their own interests.

Political beasts who are committed to ethical principles are more likely to have a positive impact on society. They are more likely to be trusted by the public, and their actions are more likely to be seen as beneficial. On the other hand, political beasts who engage in unethical behavior are more likely to be viewed with suspicion and mistrust. Their actions are more likely to be seen as harmful, and their influence may be limited as a result.

Strategies for Managing Political Beasts within Ethical Frameworks

Managing political beasts within ethical frameworks can be challenging, but there are several strategies that can be effective. One strategy is to establish clear ethical standards and hold political beasts accountable for their actions. This can be done through ethical codes of conduct, oversight committees, and other mechanisms that promote transparency and accountability.

Another strategy is to promote ethical leadership. By promoting leaders who are committed to ethical principles, political beasts are more likely to follow suit. This can be done through leadership training programs, mentoring, and other initiatives that promote ethical behavior.

Finally, promoting a culture of ethics can also be effective. When ethical behavior is valued and celebrated, political beasts are more likely to follow suit. This can be done through awareness campaigns, education, and other initiatives that promote ethical behavior and discourage unethical behavior.

In conclusion, ethics play a critical role in shaping the behavior and actions of political beasts. By promoting ethical behavior and holding political beasts accountable for their actions, we can ensure that their influence is used to advance the common good rather than harm society.

Chapter 13

Case Studies of Political Beasts in California:

Gavin Newsom: Gavin Newsom, the current Governor of California, is one of the most well-known political beasts in the state. He has been involved in California politics for over two decades and has served as the Mayor of San Francisco, Lieutenant Governor of California, and now as Governor. Newsom is known for his progressive policies and his ability to connect with younger voters. He has also been a vocal critic of former President Donald Trump.

Dianne Feinstein: Dianne Feinstein is a long-time Democratic Senator from California. She has been in office since 1992 and has been re-elected five times. Feinstein is known for her work on environmental issues, gun control, and healthcare reform. She has also been a vocal advocate for the LGBTQ+ community and women's rights.

Kamala Harris: Kamala Harris is a former Attorney General of California and a former U.S. Senator from California. She is currently serving as the Vice President of the United States. Harris is known for her progressive policies and her ability to connect with diverse communities. She has been a vocal advocate for criminal justice reform and has been a strong voice for women's rights.

Case Studies of Political Beasts in Texas:

Ted Cruz: Ted Cruz is a Republican Senator from Texas. He has been in office since 2013 and is known for his conservative policies and his strong support of the Second Amendment. Cruz has also been a vocal opponent of the Affordable Care Act and has been a strong supporter of former President Donald Trump.

Beto O'Rourke: Beto O'Rourke is a former U.S. Representative from Texas. He gained national attention during his 2018 Senate campaign against Ted Cruz. O'Rourke is known for his progressive policies and his ability to connect with younger voters. He has been a vocal advocate for gun control and has been a strong supporter of the LGBTQ+ community.

Greg Abbott: Greg Abbott is the current Governor of Texas. He has been in office since 2015 and is known for his conservative policies and his support of the Second Amendment. Abbott has also been a vocal opponent of abortion and has been a strong advocate for border security.

Case Studies of Political Beasts in New York:

Andrew Cuomo: Andrew Cuomo is a Democratic politician who served as the Governor of New York from 2011 until 2021. Cuomo is known for his strong leadership style and his ability to get things done. He has been a vocal advocate for progressive policies and has been a strong supporter of the LGBTQ+ community.

Alexandria Ocasio-Cortez: Alexandria Ocasio-Cortez is a Democratic U.S. Representative from New York. She gained national attention in 2018 when she defeated incumbent Joe Crowley in the Democratic primary. Ocasio-Cortez is known for her progressive policies and her ability to connect with younger voters. She has been a vocal advocate for climate change action and has been a strong supporter of the Green New Deal.

Chuck Schumer: Chuck Schumer is a Democratic Senator from New York. He has been in office since 1999 and has been re-elected four times. Schumer is known for his strong leadership style and his ability to get things done. He has been a vocal advocate for gun control and has been a strong supporter of the LGBTQ+ community.

Case Studies of Political Beasts in Florida:

Ron DeSantis: Ron DeSantis is the current Governor of Florida. He has been in office since 2019 and is known for his conservative policies and his support of former President Donald Trump. DeSantis has also been a vocal opponent of mask mandates and COVID-19 vaccine mandates.

Marco Rubio: Marco Rubio is a Republican Senator from Florida. He has been in office since 2011 and has been re-elected twice. Rubio is known for his conservative policies and his strong support of Israel. He has also been a vocal advocate for immigration reform and has been a strong supporter of the Cuban-American community.

Debbie Wasserman Schultz: Debbie Wasserman Schultz is a Democratic U.S. Representative from Florida. She has been in office since 2005 and has been re-elected seven times. Wasserman Schultz is known for her progressive policies and her strong advocacy for women's rights. She has also been a vocal advocate for gun control and has been a strong supporter of the LGBTQ+ community.

Overall, these political beasts in California, Texas, New York, and Florida have demonstrated their strong leadership skills, ability to connect with their constituents, and advocacy for progressive policies. Their impact on their respective states and national politics is significant and will continue to be influential in the years to come.

Chapter 14

Conclusion and Future Directions:

Political beasts have long been a feature of state politics, representing individuals who possess a unique combination of charisma, strategic thinking, and the ability to connect with voters. Their impact on state politics can be significant, shaping policies, and even influencing national politics. However, managing political beasts is an essential aspect of state politics. It is crucial to prevent their negative impact and promote policies that benefit the greater good.

The Importance of Managing Political Beasts within States:

Managing political beasts is crucial because they can manipulate public opinion and compromise the democratic process. They can sway voters to support policies that may not benefit the greater good or promote their interests, leading to a breakdown in democratic institutions. Managing political beasts requires a robust system of checks and balances, ethical leadership, and the ability to hold politicians accountable for their actions.

Future Directions for Studying Political Beasts:

The study of political beasts is crucial to understanding the dynamics of state politics. Future research should focus on developing a better understanding of the psychological traits that make individuals successful political beasts. It is also crucial to examine the cultural, economic, and social factors that influence the rise of political beasts in different states. Additionally, future research should explore the impact of social media on the ability of political beasts to sway public opinion and promote their interests.

Strategies for Preventing Political Beasts from Gaining Power:

Preventing political beasts from gaining power requires a multifaceted approach. One strategy is to promote transparency and accountability in state politics. This includes promoting ethical leadership, increasing public awareness of the political process, and strengthening democratic institutions. Another strategy is to promote the development of strong political parties that can provide an alternative to individual politicians who may become political beasts. Additionally, increasing public participation in the political process can prevent political beasts from gaining power by promoting a more diverse and inclusive political landscape.

In conclusion, managing political beasts is crucial for promoting the greater good and ensuring the democratic process remains intact. Future research should continue to explore the psychological, cultural, economic, and social factors that influence the rise of political beasts. Strategies for preventing political beasts from gaining power should focus on promoting transparency, accountability, and public participation in the political process. With the right strategies in place, the negative impact of political beasts can be minimized, and state politics can remain robust and democratic.

REFERENCES

M. E. J. Newman. Networks, An Introduction. Oxford University Press, 2010.

P. M. Baran and P. Sweezy. Monopoly Capital: An Essay on the American Economic and Social Order. Monthly Review Press, 1966.

J. S. Coleman. Foundations of Social Theory. Belknap Press, 1990.

H. White. Identity and Control: How Social Formations Emerge. Princeton University Press, 1992.

M. Granovetter. The Strength of Weak Ties. American Journal of Sociology, vol. 78, no. 6, pp. 1360–1380, 1973.

FURTHER READING:

R. Axelrod. The Evolution of Cooperation. Basic Books, 1984.

J. H. Fowler and N. A. Christakis. Cooperative behavior cascades in human social networks. Proceedings of the National Academy of Sciences, vol. 107, no. 12, pp. 5334–5338, 2010.

R. M. Emerson. Power-dependence relations. American Sociological Review, vol. 27, no. 1, pp. 31–41, 1962.

M. Brinton. The Anatomy of Revolution. Vintage, 1965.

E. Ostrom. Governing the Commons: The Evolution of Institutions for Collective Action. Cambridge University Press, 1990.

www.ingramcontent.com/pod-product-compliance
Lightning Source LLC
Chambersburg PA
CBHW061513250726
48657CB00005B/1833